Blastoff! Readers are carefully developed by literacy experts to build reading stamina and move students toward fluency by combining standards-based content with developmentally appropriate text.

LEVELS

 **Level 1** provides the most support through repetition of high-frequency words, light text, predictable sentence patterns, and strong visual support.

 **Level 2** offers early readers a bit more challenge through varied sentences, increased text load, and text-supportive special features.

 **Level 3** advances early-fluent readers toward fluency through increased text load, less reliance on photos, advancing concepts, longer sentences, and more complex special features.

★ **Blastoff! Universe**

Reading Level

 Grade K

 Grades 1–3

 Grade 4

This edition first published in 2025 by Bellwether Media, Inc.

No part of this publication may be reproduced in whole or in part without written permission of the publisher. For information regarding permission, write to Bellwether Media, Inc., Attention: Permissions Department, 6012 Blue Circle Drive, Minnetonka, MN 55343.

Library of Congress Cataloging-in-Publication Data

LC record for Belgium available at: https://lccn.loc.gov/2024012107

Text copyright © 2025 by Bellwether Media, Inc. BLASTOFF! READERS and associated logos are trademarks and/or registered trademarks of Bellwether Media, Inc. Bellwether Media is a division of Chrysalis Education Group.

Editor: Suzane Nguyen   Designer: Laura Sowers

Printed in the United States of America, North Mankato, MN.

Table of Contents

All About Belgium   4
Land and Animals   6
Life in Belgium   12
Belgium Facts   20
Glossary   22
To Learn More   23
Index   24

All About Belgium

Brussels

Belgium is a small country in Europe. Its capital is Brussels.

Belgian artists have made many characters. The Smurfs are very well known!

Land and Animals

Most of Belgium is flat and low. The northwest has **plains**.

The Ardennes is in the southeast. This hilly forest sits on a large **plateau**.

plains

Ardennes

Size: 3,860 square miles (9,997 square kilometers)

Famous For: a large forest that spreads into Belgium and two other countries

winter

Belgium is a **temperate** country. Summers are warm. Winters are cool and wet.

The country gets a lot of rain. Fog often covers the land.

fog

Most animals live in the Ardennes. Wild boars run in the forest. Newts live in the soil.

palmate newt

Red deer eat flowers. Wildcats hunt mice!

Life in Belgium

Most Belgians are Flemish or Walloon. Many are **Roman Catholic**.

People speak Dutch or French. A small group speaks German.

Roman Catholic church

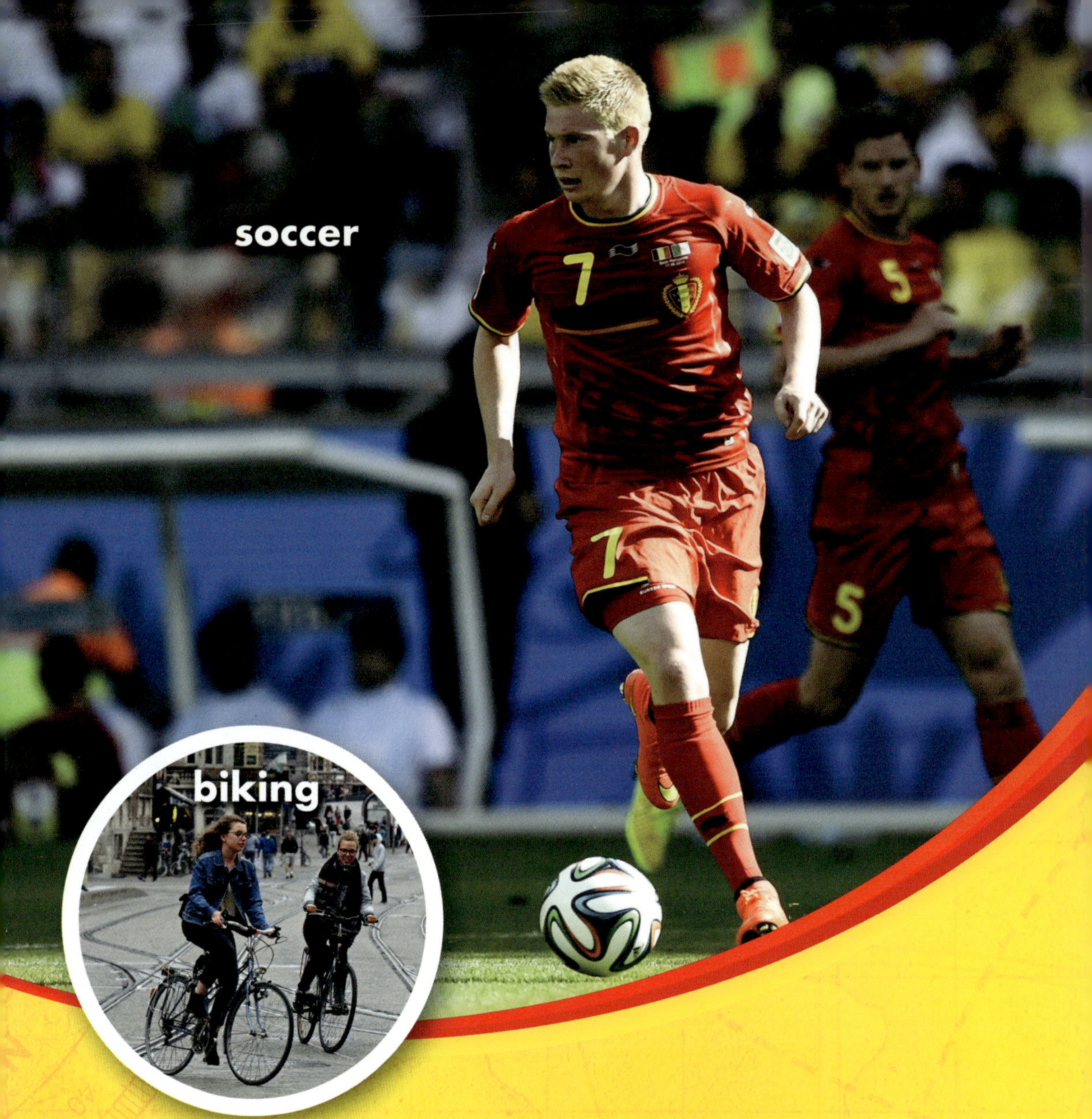

soccer

biking

Soccer is popular in Belgium. Many people also enjoy biking.

Belgians are proud of their art **culture**. They have a lot of artists. Music events take place each year.

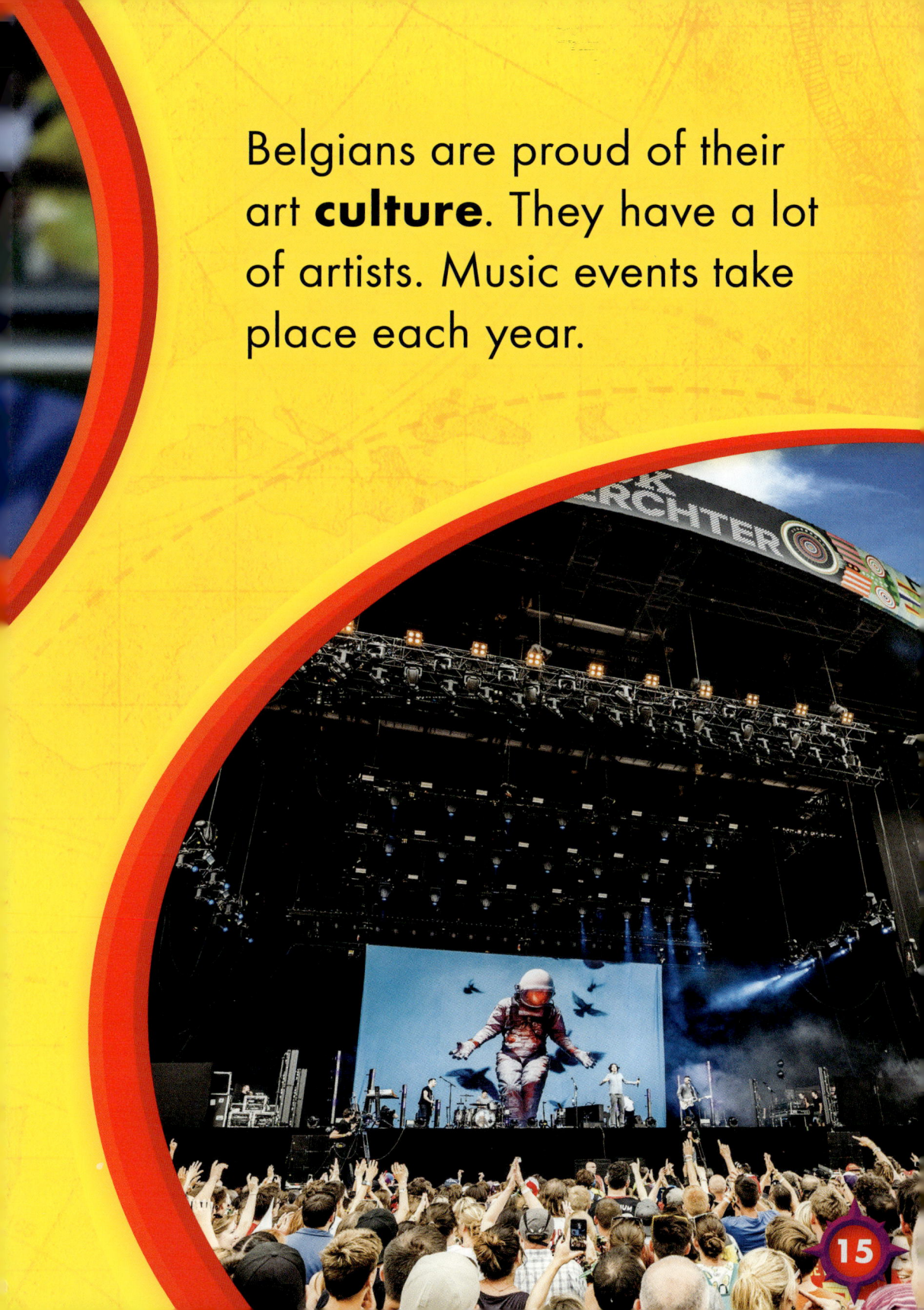

Moules frites are popular. They are **mussels** with french fries. *Carbonnade flamande* is beef stew.

Belgian Foods

moules frites

carbonnade flamande

waffles

Belgian chocolate

People eat waffles as a snack. Belgian chocolate is tasty!

The Carnival of Binche lasts for three days. People wear colorful costumes.

July 21 is Belgian National Day. People watch parades. They also enjoy fireworks. Belgians honor their country!

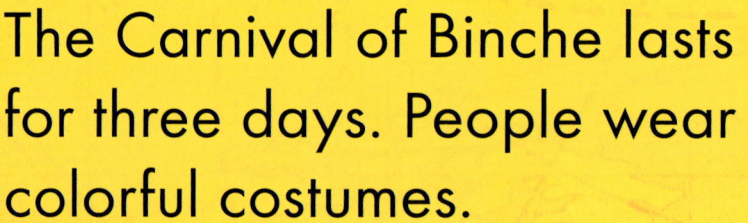

Carnival of Binche

Belgian National Day

Belgium Facts

Size:
11,787 square miles
(30,528 square kilometers)

Population:
11,913,633 (2023)

National Holiday:
Belgian National Day (July 21)

Main Languages:
Dutch, French, German

Capital City:
Brussels

Famous Face

Name: Romelu Lukaku

Famous For: soccer player and top goal scorer for the Belgian national team

Religions

- other 2%
- Roman Catholic 57%
- none 29%
- Muslim 7%
- other Christian 5%

Top Landmarks

Antwerp Central Station

Grand-Place

Hallerbos forest

Glossary

culture—the beliefs, arts, and ways of life in a place or society

mussels—animals that live in water and have dark outer shells

plains—areas of flat land with few trees

plateau—a flat, raised area of land

Roman Catholic—people belonging or relating to the Christian church that is led by the pope

temperate—related to a mild climate that does not have extreme heat or cold

To Learn More

AT THE LIBRARY

Morlock, Rachael. *Belgium*. New York, N.Y.: Cavendish Square Publishing, 2022.

Phillips-Bartlett, Rebecca. *A Visit to Belgium*. Minneapolis, Minn.: Bearport Publishing Company, 2023.

Sabelko, Rebecca. *France*. Minneapolis, Minn.: Bellwether Media, 2023.

ON THE WEB

Factsurfer.com gives you a safe, fun way to find more information.

1. Go to www.factsurfer.com.

2. Enter "Belgium" into the search box and click 🔍.

3. Select your book cover to see a list of related content.

Index

animals, 10, 11
Ardennes, 6, 7, 10
artists, 5, 15
Belgian National Day, 18, 19
Belgium facts, 20–21
biking, 14
Brussels, 4, 5
capital (see Brussels)
Carnival of Binche, 18
Dutch, 12, 13
Europe, 4
fog, 9
food, 16, 17
forests, 6, 10
French, 12
German, 12
map, 5
music, 15
people, 5, 12, 14, 15, 17, 18

plains, 6
plateau, 6
rain, 9
Roman Catholic, 12
say hello, 13
Smurfs, 5
soccer, 14
summers, 8
winters, 8

The images in this book are reproduced through the courtesy of: Sergii Figurnyi, front cover, p. 21 (Grand-Palace); Mini Onion, p. 3; Adisa, pp. 4-5; kristof lauwers, p. 6; Sophie Lenoir, pp. 6-7; Botond Horvath, pp. 8-9; Studio-Annika, p. 9; ClarkWarren1991, pp. 10-11; David Kalosson, p. 11 (wild boar); asturfauna, p. 11 (Palmate newt); Keith Hider, p. 11 (red deer); WildMedia, p. 11 (European wildcat); Mikhail Markovskiy, p. 12; Juriaan Wossink/ Alamy, pp. 12-13; Nestor Martinez Nieva, p. 14 (biking); Celso Pupo, pp. 14-15; Ben Houdijk p. 15; Chatham172, p. 16 (*moules frites*); from my point of view, p. 16 (*carbonnade flamande*); BLGKV, p. 16 (waffles); Regien Paassen, pp. 16 (Belgian chocolate), 21 (Hallerbos Forest); Bricolage, p. 17; Yaacov Dagan/ Alamy, p. 18; Andrew Wilson/ Alamy, pp. 18-19; J_UK, p. 20 (flag); Ettore Griffoni, p. 20 (Romelu Lukaku); Olgysha, p. 21 (Antwerp Central Station); Eric Isselee, p. 22.